This book belongs to

....

Consultant Sarah Davis is a (UKCP Registered) psychotherapist with an MA in Integrative Child and Adolescent Psychotherapy and Counseling.

She currently works in the voluntary sector, counseling and supporting young people to improve their mental wellbeing. She has also worked as a children's editor and consultant.

Published in 2022 by Welbeck Children's Books
An imprint of Welbeck Children's Limited, part of Welbeck Publishing Group.
Based in London and Sydney
www.welbeckpublishing.com

Text and illustrations © Welbeck Children's Limited, part of Welbeck Publishing Group.

Art Director: Margaret Hope
Designer: Nancy Leschnikoff
Editor: Jenni Lazell

All rights reserved. No part of this publication may be reproduced, stored in a retrieval system, or transmitted in any form or by any means, electronically, mechanical, photocopying, recording or otherwise, without the prior permission of the copyright owners and the publishers.

ISBN 978-1-78312-756-6

Printed in Dongguan, China
10 9 8 7 6 5 4 3 2 1

Find your COURAGE

Skolstrejk för Klimatet

Catherine Veitch, with
Sarah Davis, child and adolescent psychotherapist
Illustrated by Jessica Smith

WELBECK

CONTENTS

Getting started	6
What is courage?	8
Daring to be courageous	9
Stepping stones to courage	10
Learning courage	12
Confidence boost	13
Confidence charge	14
Build a self-esteem mountain	16
Things I love about myself	18
Pass on the compliments	19
So many decisions	20
Decision dice	22
Learning new things	24
Comfort and courage circles	25
Bucket list bingo	26
Courageous role models	28
My courageous role model	30
Bee-ing positive	31
Positive pathways	32
Positive affirmation cards	34
Body language	38
Funny faces	40
Step into your power	41
Failing is part of success	42
My worry hill	44
Sharing and caring	46
Pack up your inner strengths	48
Your inner and outer animals	49
The science of courage and fear	52
Ways to strengthen your courage muscles	54
Pop your fear	55

Feeling scared	56	Stand out from the crowd	80
Pesky phobias	58	Follow your heart	82
And breathe...	60	Courageous love	83
Breathing exercises	61	Courageous role models	84
Mindfulness and meditation	62	Get curious	86
Yoga	64	Brain teasers	88
Challenge your fears	66	Say no to bullies	94
Write away your worries	67	Dare to be different	96
Blow away your worries	68	Courageous role models	100
Create a chill-out den	70	True or false?	102
Picture it	74	My courage diary	106
My happy place	75	Courage awards	110
Time to talk about...	76	Check your answers	111
Bridge of courage	78	Further resources	112

GETTING STARTED

This book is full of ideas and activities to help improve your courage. You can work through them in order or pick out pages at random, depending on how you feel. Before you start, here's a quick introduction to the topic of courage.

Life is full of ups and downs, including joyous highs as well as moments of worry or sadness, uncertainty or confusion. But one thing is certain—there is no avoiding fear in our quest for happiness or success. Which is why courage is one of the most powerful feelings for us to learn. And it's important because it involves building and harnessing our mental tools to do something, even when we feel afraid.

There are lots of different types of courage, from overcoming a fear of spiders, to taking an exam, to standing up for something or someone you really believe in, even when it's not popular. Courage is not about perfection or being the best, though sometimes it might look like that from the outside. Courage is about taking those first small steps towards something that might feel uncomfortable and knowing that something amazing might come at the end of it.

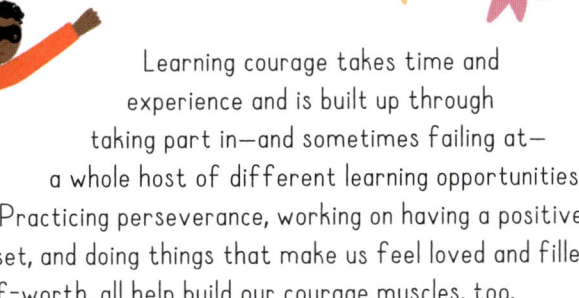

Learning courage takes time and experience and is built up through taking part in—and sometimes failing at— a whole host of different learning opportunities. Practicing perseverance, working on having a positive mindset, and doing things that make us feel loved and filled up with self-worth, all help build our courage muscles, too.

So, anything you can do to start working with your fears and stepping outside of your comfort zone right away is worth it! The more things you try, the more twists and turns you add to the exciting adventure of your life!

Now let's get started on finding out how to be *more courageous!*

WHAT IS COURAGE?

What does being courageous mean to you?

A gymnast doing a somersault off the bars, speaking in front of the whole school, or dealing with an illness? All of these things take courage, but there are also many smaller things that you may do day-to-day that are courageous. Such as schecking up for a friend who is being picked on, admitting that you need help with something, or learning to swim.

Being courageous is more than just doing something brave—it's doing something brave, even though you feel anxious about it. Even a gymnast may be scared the first time they learn a new skill—and they may still feel scared every time they perform, but they dig deep and find the courage to do it. Just as you may have worried about asking for help, but you faced your fears and did it! Courage is taking action, despite feeling scared.

Color all the words that describe how you feel when you act courageously. Add some words of your own if they are missing.

brave · daring · fearless
heroic · spirited · gutsy · nervous
powerful · bold
confident · strong · adventurous

DARING TO BE COURAGEOUS

Do you sometimes feel that you are stuck in a rut?

If you let your fears get the better of you, being scared can stop you from having the courage to embrace new opportunities, which can hold you back in life. It is not always easy to be courageous, especially if you are not used to it. But the good news is that there are ways that you can work on your courage muscles.

Here are some well-known sayings that describe what it feels like to be courageous.

PUT ON A BRAVE FACE

KEEP YOUR CHIN UP

NERVES OF STEEL

WHO DARES WINS

FACE YOUR FEARS

TAKE HEART

Think of a time when you had the courage of a lion and make up a saying to describe what it felt like to you.

STEPPING STONES TO COURAGE

Do you wish you were braver, that doing new things didn't fill you with dread, or that you had the courage to say "no" at times?

Before we start building our courage muscles, making a list of things you would like to be braver at is a good starting point for your journey, as it will give you some goals to aim for. Write down ten things that you want to be more courageous at in the stepping stones, starting with small things and building up to bigger things.

LEARNING COURAGE

So how do you build your courage muscles? Here are some tools that will help you to become less fearful and more courageous.

MANAGING FEAR AND ANXIETY

Firstly, recognize that fear is not all bad, as in situations of real danger, such as facing a polar bear, fear kick-starts your nervous system and survival instincts that may save your life. On a less dramatic scale, don't be so hard on yourself if you feel fearful and anxious when you try new things. Those feelings are expected and even the most confident people have them (they are just good at hiding them!). Fear is handy as it slows you down and makes you look at all the risks involved, which isn't a bad thing. You will find that the more often you get used to making decisions and taking risks, the more you face your fears, the less scary they will be and the more courageous you will feel.

WHO IS MANAGING THEIR FEARS BETTER?

A POSITIVE MIND

Look at your fears as an opportunity to learn something about a situation, or yourself. Try putting into words the things that scare you and you will already be on your way to being courageous, as it is brave to admit your vulnerabilities like this. Look at any failures as a chance to grow as a person. Even if you do not succeed this time, be proud as you have stepped out of your comfort zone and taken risks, despite feeling so scared.

CONFIDENCE BOOST

Try focusing on things that you are good at, which are your strengths, instead of obsessing over the things you struggle with. You are more likely to take risks and be courageous with things you can do well, so knowing your strengths will boost your confidence. As your confidence and trust in your own abilities grows, you will feel empowered and in a better place to step out of your comfort zone and chase opportunities.

STEPPING OUT OF YOUR COMFORT ZONE
Stepping out of your comfort zone and trying new things broadens the experiences you have in your life and makes you a more well-rounded person. But sometimes you need to give yourself a little push. However, if the thought of moving out of your comfort zone fills you with fear and dread, try taking small steps to begin with. Practice being courageous by tackling small fears at first. Then as you gain confidence, you will find it easier to take on bigger, more scary things.

CONFIDENCE CHARGE

A confident person believes and trusts in their abilities. When you believe in yourself you are more willing to be brave and try new things. The more confident you feel, the more courageous you will be.

Draw a time when you experienced something new and felt scared, but acted with confidence. It may have been moving to a new home or school, learning an instrument, or taking part in a competition.

How did it feel to step out of your comfort zone despite feeling scared? Remember that feeling next time you feel scared when facing something new.

As you color in this person, feel yourself being charged up with confidence!

BUILD A SELF-ESTEEM MOUNTAIN

Self-esteem is important as it helps us to value ourselves and increases our confidence.

Say these phrases out loud at times when you doubt yourself.

THINGS I LOVE ABOUT MYSELF

Do you find it hard to accept a compliment from someone and struggle with low self-esteem? One way to improve that is to focus on positive things you like about yourself rather than going over the things you don't like.

Write eight things you love about yourself in the mirror. Your challenge is that you can't say anything about your appearance, so think about your personality and things you can do well.

PASS ON THE COMPLIMENTS

Just as it's nice to receive compliments from others, it's also nice to give them. Fill in these compliment cards, and show them to the people they are for. How good does that make you feel?

Compliment card

To: _____

Something I like about you:
_____
_____
_____
_____
_____

Compliment card

To: _____

Something I like about you:
_____
_____
_____
_____
_____

Compliment card

To: _____

Something I like about you:
_____
_____
_____
_____
_____

SO MANY DECISIONS

We make hundreds of decisions every day of our lives. Such as what clothes shall I wear today, should I take an umbrella in case it rains, what shall I have for lunch? We make many simple decisions without thinking, but bigger decisions can be tricky, especially when they involve risks and can make us feel uncomfortable.

Making tricky decisions, such as choosing to join a club, or whether to put your name down for a school play, takes courage and practice. Sometimes you may make the wrong decision. But making wrong decisions is all part of growing up, and you can learn strategies to help you. The more you practice, the better you will become at making decisions.

1. Sleep on it

2. Do something else

3. Look at it in a different way

4. Imagine what someone else would do

5. List the pros and cons

1. Rather than worrying non-stop about the problem, go to bed and let your brain work on it while you are sleeping.

 2. Take your mind off the worry and do something different. You'll be surprised at what solutions your brain comes up with!

3. Can you look at the issue in a different way? For example, can you argue the opposite?

 4. Imagine how someone you admire would solve the problem.

List all of the pros (advantages) and the cons (disadvantages) for each of your choices.

1. ....

2. ....

3. ....

4. ....

DECISION DICE

Are you pondering over something at this very moment? Why not make this decision dice for a fun way to help you with the decision.

Write what you need to make a decision about here. It will help to write it as a question.

....

....

....

....

How to play

1. Copy the dice template opposite and scheck it on card.

2. Think of six different answers to your question and write each answer on a side of the dice.

3. Carefully score all of the lines and fold the sides into a cube.

4. Add some glue on the tabs to fix the sides together.

5. Now you are ready to say your question out loud and roll the dice for the answer.

fold on dotted lines and glue shaded areas

This is only a fun game so don't take the answer to heart. But notice how you feel when you get the answer to your question. If you feel anxious or disappointed about an answer, then maybe that choice is not the right one for you.

LEARNING NEW THINGS

Did you know that every time you do something new or different your brain grows? It doesn't get any bigger, but when you learn new skills, new pathways are created in your brain.

Trying new things can be scary, but try not to put pressure on yourself to be amazing at something you've never tried before and just have fun with it. You will find that your confidence grows the more you give new things a go. The more new things you learn, the more empowered you feel and you will be prepared for unexpected opportunities that come your way.

COMFORT AND COURAGE CIRCLES

Look at the things in these comfort and courage circles. Learning new things takes place in your courage circle.

COURAGE CIRCLE — Things I have never tried, Things I find difficult, Anything new, Challenges, Things I need courage to do.

COMFORT CIRCLE — Things I enjoy doing, Things I usually do, Feeling safe, Things I know, Friends I am comfortable with

Complete your own Comfort and Courage Circle. Fill in some things you do when you are in your comfort zone, and list new things you have done or would like to do in your courage circle.

COURAGE CIRCLE

COMFORT CIRCLE

25

BUCKET LIST BINGO

Play this game with one other person. Each make a list of twelve things for your bucket list. A bucket list is a list of things you want to do in your life. Check back at things you wrote in your courage circle for ideas. They can be small things, such as trying a new hairstyle, or as huge as climbing Mount Everest! There are no limits and any dream is valid. Choose a bingo board each, and write or draw your bucket list in each of the bingo squares. Now you are ready to play Bucket List Bingo!

2	3	4	5
6	7	8	9
10	11	12	ANY DOUBLE

You will need:
24 buttons or coins (12 each) to cover the squares
2 dice
Your bingo boards

How to play

1 Take it in turns to throw two dice and cover the square on your board with the same number as the total of the two dice. If a square is already covered, the turn passes to the other player.
2 If you throw the same number with each dice, you can cover the "Any double" square.
3 The winner is the player who is the first to cover all of their twelve squares.

COURAGEOUS ROLE MODELS

Other people can be role models who inspire us to be courageous by their actions. Here are some courageous people.

Name: Greta Thunberg
Born: Sweden, 2003
Role: climate change activist

Greta's story:
As a child, Greta worried about climate change destroying her future. She decided to do something about it and went on a school strike. Every Friday, Greta skipped school and sat down in front of the Swedish parliament with her banner "School strike for the climate." Her protest sparked other protests all around the world and her message that we have to act now to stop climate change was brought to the world's attention.

Giving back: Greta has been diagnosed with Asperger's Syndrome and is painfully shy, but she doesn't let that hold her back. She is so passionate about making a difference that she speaks at huge public gatherings and has met many world leaders.

Name: Carlos Acosta
Born: Cuba, 1973
Role: world-famous ballet dancer and director

Carlos's story:
Carlos's family were poor when he was growing up. He lived in a one-bedroom apartment with his parents and ten siblings, with no running water. Carlos spent a lot of time hanging out on the streets. His father was worried that Carlos would fall in with the wrong crowd, so he signed him up for ballet school. At first Carlos didn't like ballet, bunking off to breakdance on the streets and play soccer. But he eventually got the ballet bug and put in years of hard work to become the world-famous ballet dancer and director he is today.

Giving back: Carlos remembered how he struggled growing up, so he set up the Carlos Acosta International Dance Foundation to give young dancers more of a chance to make something of their lives.

Name: Professor Stephen Hawking
Born: UK, 1942
Role: physicist, cosmologist, mathematician, and author

Stephen's story:
Stephen was incredibly smart. He won a scholarship to study physics at Oxford University where he achieved a first-class degree (the highest grade!), then he went on to study cosmology, or how the universe works, at Cambridge University. But at 21, Stephen discovered he had motor neurone disease, which affected his movement, including his walking and talking. There was no cure. When Stephen's condition worsened, he had to use a wheelchair and a computer to speak. But Stephen didn't let that stop him and he continued studying and went on to make many discoveries about the universe.

Giving back: Stephen wrote a number of science books about the universe that explained concepts clearly, so more people could understand them. He has given the world a better understanding of space and time, especially black holes, and changed what we know in physics.

Name: Malala Yousafzai
Born: Pakistan, 1997
Role: campaigner for girls' education

Malala's story: In Pakistan, where Malala grew up, many children didn't have the chance to go to school. It was especially difficult for girls. Malala was lucky, as her parents valued education for all children and her father set up a school for girls. However, when new rulers took charge where Malala lived, they made a law that girls could not go to school. Malala spoke out in public saying that girls had a right to learn. When she was 15 years old, masked gunmen burst onto her school bus and shot her in the head. Malala was sent to a hospital in England. After months of surgeries and getting better, Malala's family joined her in the UK, where she continued with her education.

Giving back: Malala set up the Malala Fund, which is a charity dedicated to giving every girl the opportunity to go to school. Malala continues to speak up for girls around the world, traveling to many countries and listening to their stories of poverty, war, child marriage and fighting for the right to go to school.

MY COURAGEOUS ROLE MODEL

Do you have a courageous role model? It may be someone in your family, a teacher or a friend, or even a character in a book or movie. Draw a picture of them, and fill in a fact file to show why they are your role model.

Name:
Born:
Role:

Story:

Giving back:

BEE-ING POSITIVE

Being positive can help us to be more courageous. We all have disappointments, which we have no control over, but we can control how we react to them. That is, we can choose to react negatively or positively.

A negative reaction would be to let the disappointment get you down and think that you are no good. But a positive reaction would be to ask yourself what you have learned and what you can do differently to change things for next time. Don't worry if you find it hard to keep positive. The good news is that we can train our brains to replace negative thoughts with positive thoughts. And the more you practice, the easier being positive will become.

Just using positive language can change your brain and put you in a more positive mood. Positive language focuses on what can be done, suggests choices, and is encouraging. Whereas negative language focuses on what can't be done and emphasizes negative consequences. Look at how these negative phrases have been turned into positive ones.

Don't walk on the grass	Please walk on the paths
I forgot	I'll set a reminder next time
I can't do this	I'll ask for help
I don't like vegetables	I'll try some vegetables, as I may find I like them
I'm fed up	What other things can I do today?

POSITIVE PATHWAYS

Your brain may look like a giant sponge, but it's actually made up of billions of nerve cells called neurons.

These neurons "talk" to each other along pathways every time you do something—it all happens super-quick and without you realizing. Focusing on positive words and phrases helps to create positive pathways in your brain.

Color in all the positive neurons to creative a positive pathway across this brain. The first and last neurons have been colored.

I CAN'T

IT'S YOUR FAULT

WILL DO

START

YES

GO FOR IT!

POSITIVE is encouraging.

POSITIVE says what can be done.

NEGATIVE says the consequences.

POSITIVE AFFIRMATION CARDS

Positive affirmations are a great way to switch your brain from negative thinking to positive thinking. If you repeat them enough, your brain starts to believe them.

Make some positive affirmation cards to say out loud every day. Color in these cards and write some positive statements on them. Use some of the options below or make up some of your own.

I am kind

I am loved

All is well

I am a good friend

I am safe

I am grateful

I can do anything

I am ready to try new things

I can find solutions

I am happy

I belong

I AM KIND.

I belong.

"One child, one teacher, one book, one pen can change the world."

— Malala Yousafzai

Let your mind wander and fill this space with happy things.

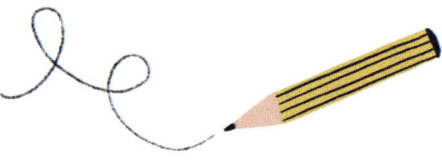

STRONG COLORING

Imagine you are as strong as a tree, with roots anchoring you to the ground as you color.

BODY LANGUAGE

Our body language describes how we hold our bodies, the gestures we make and the expressions on our faces. Did you know that you can boost your self-esteem by changing your body language?

Have you noticed how when you are feeling brave you stand tall, pull your shoulders back, lift your chin, look straight ahead, and use a strong voice? We will call this the power pose. And when you are feeling scared, you shrink back and talk with a quiet voice. Just changing how you hold your body can make you think and feel different. For example, if you need to speak up in front of the class, try standing in a power pose, even if you don't feel powerful, and see if it helps you to find some inner strength to speak out.

shoulders down and standing tall shows you are confident and relaxed

a big smile and an open posture shows you are happy and relaxed

looking straight ahead and direct eye contact shows you are engaged

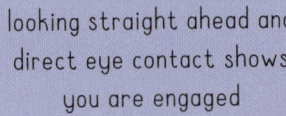

Look at these different types of body language and what they might mean. It's fun to guess people's body language, but try not to pick things apart one by one and make hasty judgements. Instead look at the body language all together, along with what the person is saying and the situation.

As well as helping our confidence, our body language is the first thing other people notice about us and positive body language helps us to make a good first impression. Understanding other people's body language also helps us to communicate with them better.

eyebrows coming together and pointing upwards, with a wrinkled mouth can show you are stressed or anxious

hands on hips and a down-turned mouth can make you look aggressive

looking away can show you are uncomfortable or not interested

If you notice that much of your body language is negative, try changing it to more positive body language. Start by changing one thing at a time, and with practice you will improve your body language skills.

FUNNY FACES

Add some expressions to these faces to match the emotions. Think about the body language of the eyes and the mouth.

happy

sad

anxious

angry

frightened

shocked

STEP INTO YOUR POWER

Draw yourself standing in a power pose ready to take on the world. Look at the tips for how to stand.

chin up

shoulders down

don't fidget

stand up straight

look ahead

Practice Feeling Powerful: Stand in your power pose and say some positive affirmations at the start of each day.

FAILING IS PART OF SUCCESS

We have all experienced failure at some point in our lives. For example, have you ever lost at a game, scored badly in an exam, or answered a question incorrectly? It doesn't feel nice to fail. But failure is really important and is a part of success.

Courage helps us to build resilience and to dig deep and keep going after failure. Ask yourself what things you have learned from a failure. Can you make a plan for next time, rather than dwelling on your mistakes? Are there any things you could do differently to change the result?

WAYS TO BOUNCE BACK AFTER FAILURE

- THINK POSITIVELY
- BELIEVE IN YOURSELF
- TAKE CARE OF YOURSELF
- STEP OUT OF YOUR COMFORT ZONE

Everyone experiences failure. If these well-known people had given up after failing, they would not have achieved all they did.

J. K. Rowling's *Harry Potter* stories were rejected twelve times before a publisher accepted them. If J. K. Rowling had given up after any one of those rejections, the *Harry Potter* stories would not have been published.

Some great inventors have discovered things by making mistakes. For example, scientist Alexander Fleming returned to his laboratory after a two-week holiday to discover that dirt had accidentally got onto a dish, and mold was now growing on the dish. Fleming investigated this and noticed that the mold killed the bacteria around it. He had discovered the drug penicillin, a medicine that is used to treat bacterial infections today. If Fleming had given up and thrown the dish away when he found the mold, we would not have life-saving penicillin.

MY WORRY HILL

Do you find that when you worry about something rather than facing it, the worry gets worse? By avoiding things we are scared of we never get the chance to be courageous and challenge the fear, or find out that we can actually cope with it.

Facing your fears is a bit like riding up a big hill. The worry grows as you ride uphill, but if you keep going and don't give up, once you get to the top of the hill and face your fear in a safe way, you will find it's an easy ride down. So, jump on your bicycle and let's tackle this worry hill together, following the five steps in CLIMB. Write your worry on the hill and imagine you are riding the bicycle.

C

Call out your worry, and see it as unrealistic. You may say "That's my worry talking, not me."
Check the box when you've done this.

L

Look your worry in the face and tell it you are in charge. You may say "I am in charge and not you, worry."
Check the box when you've done this.

These things will also help you to face your fears:

Mindfulness

Breathing exercises

Yoga

Support

Positive affirmations

I am worried about:

_____

_____

I

Ignore what your worry is telling you. You may say "I am not going to do what you want." Check the box when you've done this.

☐

M

Me-time. Enjoy your success and reward yourself. You may say "I am proud of myself for having courage." Check the box when you've done this.

☐

B

Bravo! You did it, and you can do it again! Check the box to congratulate yourself.

☐

SHARING AND CARING

Humans are social animals and, just like we need food and shelter to survive, we also need each other. Other people are important as they support us and give us the courage to do things. However, some people prefer to be alone, and if this is you, that is okay too.

We find connections and a feeling of belonging with other people in different groups or communities. For example, you may find belonging with friends, family, at school, in clubs, with religious groups, in sport teams or on social media. Some people make connections in small groups, and others feel connections to people all over the world. A crisis like the COVID-19 pandemic, where we could not mix with others, showed us how important the communities we belong to are for our happiness.

Write some of the groups you belong to in the hands.

Feeling that we belong is important for our mental and physical health and wellbeing. Belonging to a community—such as your family, friends, or school—can help you by:

- Making you feel safe
- Listening to your problems and supporting you by helping find solutions
- Giving your life a purpose through shared interests

Some people struggle with finding communities to join and may be lonely. If you struggle to fit in, here are some things that may help:

☆ Find activities and groups of people with the same interests as you. Also be open-minded and say yes to things you wouldn't normally consider. You may find that you really enjoy something unexpected! Focus on similarities that connect you to others (not on the differences) and be open to new ways of thinking.

☆ Be patient: it sometimes takes time to feel comfortable in a new group.

☆ Stay in touch: once you build friendships in a group, make an effort to keep them.

☆ If you are still struggling to fit in, don't be afraid to ask for help from a trusted adult or friend. We all need help at times.

PACK UP YOUR INNER STRENGTHS

Just as other people give us support and help us to have courage, we can also find strength inside ourselves.

What words would you use to describe your inner strength? Write these words in the backpack—you may use some of the words on this page, or choose different words.

We can work on and build our inner strength.

DETERMINED

common sense

firm

STUBBORN

kind

funny

confidence

PURPOSEFUL

integrity

PLUCKY

cool

GRITTY

BACKBONE

self-belief

PERSEVERING

YOUR INNER AND OUTER ANIMALS

What animal best describes your inner strength?
What animal best describes you on the outside?
Draw these animals, one inside the other.

"You are never too small to make a difference."

— Greta Thunberg

Use this space to write any other inspiring quotes that you find or make up some of your own.

POWERFUL COLORING

Step into your lion power and bring this lion to life with your brightest colors.

THE SCIENCE OF COURAGE AND FEAR

Courage doesn't always feel like courage. From the outside courage may look like a lion: magnificent and powerful. But on the inside, you may feel scared and full of self-doubt. Courage and fear always go together, as without fear, there is no need for courage.

What happens in your brain when you are faced with something scary? It can be something big, such as a tiger on the loose, or something small, such as doing something on your own. As soon as you are faced with something scary, a small organ in the middle of your brain, called the amygdala, gets to work.

The amygdala sends out messages to other parts of your brain that tell you how to react. The way you react is called fight or flight. You either stay and deal with the fear, or run from it. Stress hormones, such as cortisol and adrenaline, are also released in the brain, which make different things happen in your body such as sweaty palms and a quicker heartbeat.

The amygdala was very useful when we lived over two million years ago as cave people and faced many dangers, but today we do not always need to fight or run from things. Often our brains overreact and we get stressed over small things. One way of dealing with this is to work out what you are really scared of, and to try looking at it in a different way.

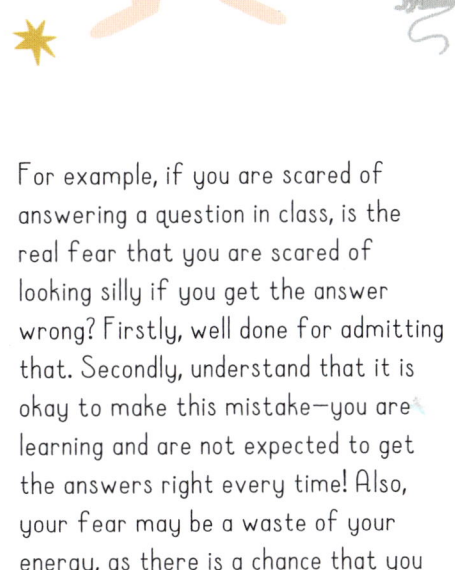

For example, if you are scared of answering a question in class, is the real fear that you are scared of looking silly if you get the answer wrong? Firstly, well done for admitting that. Secondly, understand that it is okay to make this mistake—you are learning and are not expected to get the answers right every time! Also, your fear may be a waste of your energy, as there is a chance that you may get the answer right!

WAYS TO STRENGTHEN YOUR COURAGE MUSCLES

1. If safe to do so, face your fears over and over again. This builds up the memory of the experience in your body. So if you come across the situation again you will have a better idea of how to handle it, and you will also know that you CAN cope with it.

2. Look at how you react to your fear in a different way. For example, if you get sweaty palms and a fast heartbeat, don't tell yourself that means you are scared, but say to yourself that means you are excited to be doing something out of your comfort zone and give yourself the chance to create something new in your life. This change of perspective creates new pathways in your brain.

3. Focus on the experience rather than the outcome. For example, learning to play the piano (the experience) may scare you because you are worried about passing the exams or playing in front of people (the outcome). This fear may stop you from learning to play altogether. Rather than worrying about the exams or the performance, which are a long way off as you are only a beginner, just enjoy learning to play, one small note at a time.

POP YOUR FEAR

Sometimes our fears can start out small, but if they're not addressed, can get bigger and bigger. Are you ready to pop your fear? Inflate a balloon and use a marker pen to write down your fears. On the other side of the balloon, write down the first step you are going to take to address your fear.

When you are ready, take a pin and POP your fear balloon!

You can also blow soap bubbles while thinking of your fear and watch as they fall to the ground and POP!

I am scared of spiders

FEELING SCARED

As we have found out, different things make us scared. Sometimes they are real threats, such as a hurricane or a bear on the loose. But often we are scared by things we imagine are threats, even though our life is not in any danger. Our bodies still react to the imagined threats as if they are real.

What things happen to your body when you are scared? Can you feel your heart beating faster? Do you have sweaty palms? Many changes happen in our bodies as we prepare to deal with threats. When you are afraid, your lungs take in air faster to supply your body with oxygen. Your heart rate increases to pump more blood to your muscles and your brain. The pupils in your eyes get larger so you can see better. Even your digestive system slows down temporarily so you can concentrate on more important things.

Color in the things you have felt when you have been scared:

- dry mouth
- feel sick
- chills
- shaking
- upset tummy
- pounding heart
- sweating
- short of breath

PESKY PHOBIAS

Some people have an exaggerated and unrealistic fear of something. This kind of extreme fear is called a phobia. For example, people may have phobias of spiders, the dark, or monsters under the bed. These things are not a real threat, but the person who has them sees them as that. Phobias are not pleasant and can feel overwhelming.

If you or anyone you know suffers from phobias, let's blast those pesky phobias off into space... Draw your phobias inside the rocket. Hurry, as it's taking off!

Hairyphobia

BLACK HOLE

Make up a name for each phobia. Look at some of these real names of phobias (and what they are a fear of) for ideas. Some phobias may seem strange, but they are real to the person who suffers from them.

Agoraphobia (open spaces)
Nyctophobia (dark)
Cynophobia (dogs)
Octophobia (the number 8)
Genuphobia (knees)
Scolionophobia (school)

AND BREATHE...

Breathing is essential for life as our bodies need oxygen to survive. When we breathe in, oxygen goes into our bloodstream. As we breathe out, we get rid of the waste product, carbon dioxide.

We breathe without thinking, but when we are stressed, we often take quick, shallow breaths. This can upset the balance of oxygen and carbon dioxide in our bodies, and we don't get as much oxygen into our blood. Too little oxygen in our blood can trigger a stress reaction in our bodies. For example, it may make our hearts beat quicker, and leave us feeling dizzy and our muscles tight, which can lead to us feeling even more anxious, and even to panic attacks.

When you are feeling stressed try stepping aside and taking some slow, deep breaths to get more oxygen into your bloodstream, which will help to calm you down.

BREATHING EXERCISES

Breathing exercises can calm our minds. There are many kinds of breathing exercises that you can practice—find one that suits you. Find somewhere to sit quietly and comfortably and try these breathing exercises...

TRIANGLE BREATHING

1. Breathe in through your nose and count 3 seconds in your head. While you do this, imagine drawing the first side of a triangle.
2. Hold your breath and count 3 seconds in your head. While you do this, imagine drawing the second side of the triangle.
3. Breathe out through your mouth and count 3 seconds in your head. While you do this, imagine drawing the third side of a triangle. You have just completed one deep breath.

Repeat this a few more times to feel calm.

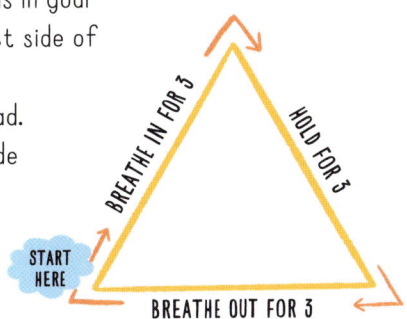

LION'S BREATH

1. Sit on your knees or cross-legged on the floor. Rest your hands on your knees, spreading your fingers out wide.
2. Breathe in through your nose.
3. Open your mouth wide and stick out your tongue as far down as it will go towards your chin.
4. Do a big breath out, forcing the air over your tongue and making a "HAA" sound that comes deep from within your tummy.
5. Breathe normally for a few moments.

Then repeat the lion's breath a few more times.

MINDFULNESS AND MEDITATION

Mindfulness is taking notice of the present moment and being aware of your thoughts, feelings and body, as well as the world around you. This will make it easier to manage your fears and practice being courageous.

When we practice mindfulness, our attention is on things right now, instead of thinking about things from the past or things coming up in the future, which can overload our minds and make us feel stressed. Practising mindfulness can change your brain pathways and help you to feel calm.

The next time you are outside, play this mindful game:

1. What four things can you see? Look up high, to the tops of trees or buildings, look behind things, look closely at things, look on the ground.
2. What four things can you hear? Are there lots of birds or people, are there different calls or voices? What sounds can you hear in the distance, and nearby?
3. What four things can you feel? What does the ground feel like under your feet—is it squelchy, soft, cold, or hard? What can you feel in your hands? Can you feel the wind, rain, or sun on your face?
4. What four things can you smell? Can you smell soil, plants, grass, the street, or people?

Each time you play the game, challenge yourself to observe different things.

EATING MINDFULLY

Next time you are eating your lunch, try eating it mindfully. Chew every bite slowly, paying attention to its taste and enjoying it. Does it taste salty, meaty, or sweet? Does it make your mouth water? How does the rest of your body feel?

MINDFUL MEDITATION

Meditation is one way to practice mindfulness.

1. Sit in a comfortable position. Gently rest your hands on your knees. Sit up straight and hold your head up, but stay relaxed.
2. Close your eyes and relax. Slowly breathe in and out. Let go of any tension in your face, your shoulders or anywhere you feel it. Pay attention to your breathing, in and out, in and out.
3. Don't worry if your mind wanders. Each time you have a thought, just imagine it floating away, and bring yourself back to focusing on your breathing.
4. After about one minute, open your eyes. How do you feel? Do you feel more relaxed? Hopefully you do, but don't worry if you don't. With practice you will learn to relax.

YOGA

Yoga exercises can calm and relax you, as well as improve your strength, concentration, balance, coordination, and flexibility. Put on some comfortable clothes and have a go at these yoga poses. Hold them for a minute if you can—and remember to breathe!

MOUNTAIN POSE
If you are having a wobbly moment and need some courage, stand tall like a mountain in this pose. Keep your back straight, your head up and your shoulders relaxed. Stand with your feet apart and hold your palms forward, with your fingers spread out.

WARRIOR POSE
Stand with your feet apart. Then turn your body and one foot forward, keeping the other foot turned in. Raise your arms and bend the knee over the foot facing forward.

TREE POSE

Stand up straight and focus on a point in front of you. Slowly bend one knee and bring up the foot. Rest it on the inside of the other leg. Stretch up your arms like the branches of a tree. If you are struggling to balance, try holding your arms out to the sides, or holding onto something to start with.

HERO POSE

Sit on your knees. Keeping your knees together, slide your feet apart so that your bottom can sit between your legs. Rest your hands on your lap. Sit up straight, keeping your shoulders pressed down.

CHILD'S POSE

Spread your knees apart, keeping the tops of your feet on the floor and your big toes touching. Bring your tummy to rest between your thighs and rest your forehead on the floor. Stretch out your arms in front of you with your palms on the floor.

If you have an injury or are worried about your health, check with a doctor before you do any of these poses. Listen to your body and if you feel any discomfort stop the exercise immediately.

CHALLENGE YOUR FEARS

Have you found that when you're drowning in your worries it's often difficult to think straight? Taking a step back from our fears, and weighing up all the evidence, helps us to put them into perspective and see that they may not be so scary.

Make a list of your fears, then put on your sensible hat and write down the evidence that challenges that fear.

My Fears	The Evidence That Challenges My Fear

WRITE AWAY YOUR WORRIES

A journal is like a diary where you write down your thoughts and feelings.

Journaling is a useful tool if you are worrying about something, as you may find that getting your worries out onto paper feels like you are letting them go. Try asking yourself lots of questions and answering them—kind of like having a conversation with yourself. You will be surprised at what things pop up, and it may help you to work things out.

> Give yourself 5 or 10 minutes and write down anything that is bothering you. Don't worry about spelling or grammar. Just let it all out. If you're not used to journaling, you may find it hard at first, but the more often you journal, the easier it becomes.

BLOW AWAY YOUR WORRIES

Your worries are just thoughts, and you are not your thoughts. Write each worrying thought on a leaf and imagine the wind blowing them away.

CREATE A CHILL-OUT DEN

We all get worried and stressed from time to time. A chill-out den, or a safe space is useful when you need some quiet time to think and reflect. Whether you need the courage to face something difficult, have already done so, or need time to relax after doing something challenging, a quiet space can restore your energy.

Use this page to plan your chill-out den and write some ideas inside the bubbles. You can use the suggestions, or make up some of your own.

bedroom ✦ garden shed ✦ tent ✦ room corner ✦ under the stairs

Where is my chill-out den?

fairy lights ✦ cushions ✦ blankets ✦ books

What will I put in my chill-out den?

photos ✦ positive affirmations ✦ plants

How will I decorate my chill-out den?

breathing exercises ✦ yoga ✦ meditation ✦ read ✦ listen to music ✦ coloring

Things I will do in my chill-out den.

"I never lose.
I either win or learn."

— Nelson Mandela

Let your mind wander and fill
this space with happy things.

COLOR AND CHILL

Chill out while you color in this beautiful sea scene.

PICTURE IT

When you use visualization, you create a mental picture in your head.

You can use visualization to give you courage and help with things that you are anxious about doing by picturing them going well before you do them. Creating a picture of a positive outcome in your head helps you to focus on the things that go right and reinforces the positives. Sports people use visualization before competing to help them do well in their events. This can work for you too.

HAPPY PLACE:
You can also use visualization to relax by creating a picture in your head of a happy place where you feel calm and relaxed. Try this exercise... and repeat it each time you need to relax.

Before you start, make sure you are sitting or lying comfortably and don't have any distractions. Turn off any devices and find a quiet place where you won't be disturbed.

- Close your eyes, slow down your breathing, and let go of any tension in your body.
- Imagine you are in a calm, relaxing place such as on a beach. Smell the salty seaweed, hear the waves gently lapping on the shore, and the cry of distant seagulls. Feel the soft sand as you sink into it, and the gentle, warm sun on your face.
- Relax your face, let go of any tension in your mouth and shoulders. Feel yourself sinking deeper into the sand as the relaxation travels down your body to your arms and hands, your tummy, your legs, and feet. Breathe in time to the waves as they roll up and down the shore.
- When you feel relaxed and ready, imagine yourself slowly waking up and walking away from the beach. Open your eyes and get up.

MY HAPPY PLACE

Draw a happy place where you feel calm and relaxed, which you can use in your visualization. It may be snuggled up with your pet on the sofa, or a favorite spot in a garden or park. Draw things that you can see, hear, smell, and touch in this place.

TIME TO TALK ABOUT...

Talking about your worries or things you want to pluck up the courage to do can help them seem more manageable and give you the strength to go for them.

Fill in these Time To Talk About speech bubbles, then talk about your answers with friends and family. Ask them the same questions.

BRIDGE OF COURAGE

There are different ways that we can be courageous.

One way is physical courage when someone does a physical action that is brave. For example, catching a spider in your room to release outside when you really don't like spiders, or a firefighter rescuing someone from a burning building.

A firefighter rescues a person from a burning building.

Write six acts of physical courage in each part of the bridge to complete the bridge.

STAND OUT FROM THE CROWD

Another type of courage is social courage. This is courage that we show when we are in a group of people.

Social courage is brave because it often means standing up for what we know is right against the rest of a group. Standing up to a group, such as your friends, may make you unpopular and make things difficult for you. Knowing this makes it hard to do, but even more courageous if you do it.

Think about the reasons why you may find it difficult to stand up to a group. Check the boxes beside any of the things you have felt, and add any other reasons.

- ☐ I want to fit in with the group.
- ☐ I want to be liked.
- ☐ I want their approval.
- ☐ I'm worried about being the next target.
- ☐ I worry about what people think.
- ☐ I'm scared of people getting angry with me.
- ☐ I don't like conflict.
- ☐ I want an easy life.

Look at the dilemmas on these Conflict Cards and fill in what happened when you faced them. If you have not experienced them, imagine how you would react and feel.

CONFLICT CARD

CONFLICT:
Someone is being bullied in the group.

MY REACTION:

REASON FOR MY ACTIONS:

HOW IT MADE ME FEEL:

CONFLICT CARD

CONFLICT:
One of my friends is cheating.

MY REACTION:

REASON FOR MY ACTIONS:

HOW IT MADE ME FEEL:

Discuss the Conflict Cards with friends and family. How different are their replies to yours?

FOLLOW YOUR HEART

Emotional courage is when you follow your heart and express how you feel even though you are afraid of the outcome, as you are not sure how someone will react or are worried about being embarrassed.

Use this space to draft a letter to someone you may have upset, or to someone who may have hurt you. Explain to them how you feel. Be honest with your feelings, but also remember to be kind. Facing things and telling someone how you really feel shows emotional courage.

Dear

From

Do you have the courage to send the letter? Talk to an adult first.

COURAGEOUS LOVE

It's often easy to take the people closest to us for granted and it can take courage to tell our friends and family how much they mean to us. Make and play this Emotional Courage game with your friends and family and let them know how special they are.

To play the game:

1. Each person has a sheet of different colored paper or card, which they tear or cut into strips.
2. Each person then writes one kind thing on each of their strips that they would like to say to each person in the game but haven't had the courage to do so. Look at the examples below for some ideas.
3. Everyone folds up their paper strips and hands them to the person they are meant for. So each person ends up with a pile of the same number of strips.
4. Take it in turns to read out the strips from your pile.

COURAGEOUS ROLE MODELS

Here are some more courageous people to inspire you with their brave actions.

Name: Jesse Martin
Born: Germany, 1981
Role: world record-breaking sailor

Jesse's story:
Jesse learned to sail on his father's catamaran boat when he was only fourteen. By seventeen, Jesse was ready to follow his dream of sailing round the world on his own. He set off in a 32 ft. sailing boat, which he called *The Lionheart*. He faced many challenges on the voyage, including hitting a whale, being knocked over countless times by huge stormy waves, and nearly colliding with a tanker. He was also often cold, scared, and alone, but he never gave up and after 328 days at sea Jesse had made it! He was the youngest person to sail non-stop around the world on his own.

Giving back: Jesse made a movie and a book—*Lionheart: A Journey of the Human Spirit*—about his adventure, which inspired other young adventurers to pursue their dreams. He showed how keeping your eye on your goals can help you to overcome challenges.

Name: Nelson Mandela
Born: South Africa, 1918
Role: anti-apartheid activist

Nelson's story:
When Nelson Mandela grew up in South Africa there was a system called apartheid, which kept black and white people apart (apartheid means "apartness"). People used different parks, buses, taxis, water fountains, and even toilets. They went to different schools and lived in different areas. The townships where the black people lived were in a terrible condition. Nelson wanted to bring the South African people together and improve conditions for black people. He took part in strikes, spoke out at rallies, and was arrested many times. Eventually he was sent to prison for life. It was a very strict prison and Nelson was only allowed one thirty-minute visit with one person each year, and could send and receive two letters a year. He was in prison for 27 years. It was only when apartheid ended that Nelson was freed. And when black people could vote along with white people, he was elected as South Africa's first black president!

Giving back: Nelson Mandela believed the apartheid system was wrong and stood up for what he believed in. He spent his life challenging racism and brought about many changes to an unfair system.

Name: Samantha Smith
Born: United States, 1972
Role: peace ambassador

Samantha's story:
Samantha grew up in a time when there were many disagreements between the United States and the Soviet Union, and the threat of a nuclear war between the countries was very real. When Samantha was ten years old she asked her mother if there was going to be a nuclear war. Her mother showed her a picture of Yuri Andropov, the leader of the Soviet Union, and told her to write and ask him. So Samantha did! Andropov replied, telling Samantha that she was courageous to write the letter and he invited her to visit the Soviet Union. Samantha and her family spent two weeks traveling around the Soviet Union meeting people, including visiting a children's camp. Samantha declared that Russian children are just like children in the United States.

Giving back: Sadly, a few years later, back in America when she was just 13 years old, Samantha and her father were killed in a plane crash. Before the fatal crash, Samantha did many television interviews and wrote a book—*Journey to the Soviet Union*—which showed people around the world how we are all the same and just want peace.

Name: George Mpanga
Born: Great Britain, 1991
Role: spoken word artist

George's story: George Mpanga was born on a tough housing estate in London, where many people were poor and children often turned to crime. With the support of his parents, George got into a good grammar school, but he felt people weren't interested in him or where he came from, which made him mad. So he began rapping to express his frustration, performing on street corners and in clubs. He won a place at Cambridge University where he took a course in spoken word poetry. He began to express his thoughts through this and made many YouTube videos, which attracted thousands of hits. He even performed in front of royalty.

Giving back: Today George performs as George the Poet and speaks out about the problems faced by poor inner-city communities, such as issues of race, class, and injustice. His poems inspire people and change many people's minds by making them sit up and listen.

GET CURIOUS

Are you curious? Do you listen to what other people have to say? Do you want to understand the reason behind things rather than just accepting them? These things show intellectual courage.

A person with intellectual courage challenges information. For example, instead of simply accepting a way of working out a maths problem, they question that way again and again, until they understand why.

Are you ready to get curious and stretch your intellectual courage?

HOW TO PLAY

1. Write something to Get Curious about on each card.
2. Tear up some paper and cover each card with a piece of paper.
3. Uncover a card at a time and do the challenge on the card.

You could ask a friend or family member to write some, too, and take it in turns to do the challenges.

Here are some examples, but write your own if you like them better:

☆ Find two different versions of a well-known story, such as a fairy tale, and spot five differences between the two.
☆ Memorize a long poem.
☆ Learn ten words in another language.
☆ Write ten questions on a topic you would like to know more about.
☆ Talk for one minute and give your opinion on something in the news.
☆ Then talk for one minute arguing against everything you have just said.

DID YOU KNOW?
In the 1600s people thought the Earth was flat, but a famous scientist called Galileo challenged that and courageously spoke out saying it was round. People mocked him, but it turned out he was right!

BRAIN TEASERS

You will need to challenge what you read and think outside the box to solve these brain teasers. Read the clues carefully and look for words that may have more than one meaning. There may be a few answers, but there is one best answer.

1. A carrot, a scarf, and four stones are found lying on a lawn. No one put them on the lawn, so why are they there?

2. A woman gave birth to two sons at the same hour, in the same month of the same year. But they were not twins. How can this be?

----

3. A man lives on the twelfth floor of an apartment block. Every day he takes the elevator down to the first floor and goes to work. When he returns he takes the elevator up to the tenth floor and then walks up the stairs the rest of the way to his home on the twelfth floor. Why does he walk part of the way up the stairs?

----

4. A lady was driving, and roared with laughter when she bumped into another car. Why did she laugh?

5. Many voices were heard coming from inside a classroom, but when the teacher checked there was only one child in there. What's going on?

----

6. Max entered a store and everyone in the store rushed out screaming. What happened?

----

7. Four children entered a classroom, but only three walked out. The classroom is empty, so where is the fourth child?

----

8. A man and his wife raced through the streets. They stopped, the husband got out of the car and left his wife. When he returned there was another person in the car with his wife. What had happened?

----

9. A child spotted a fierce tiger in the distance and ran toward it. Why?

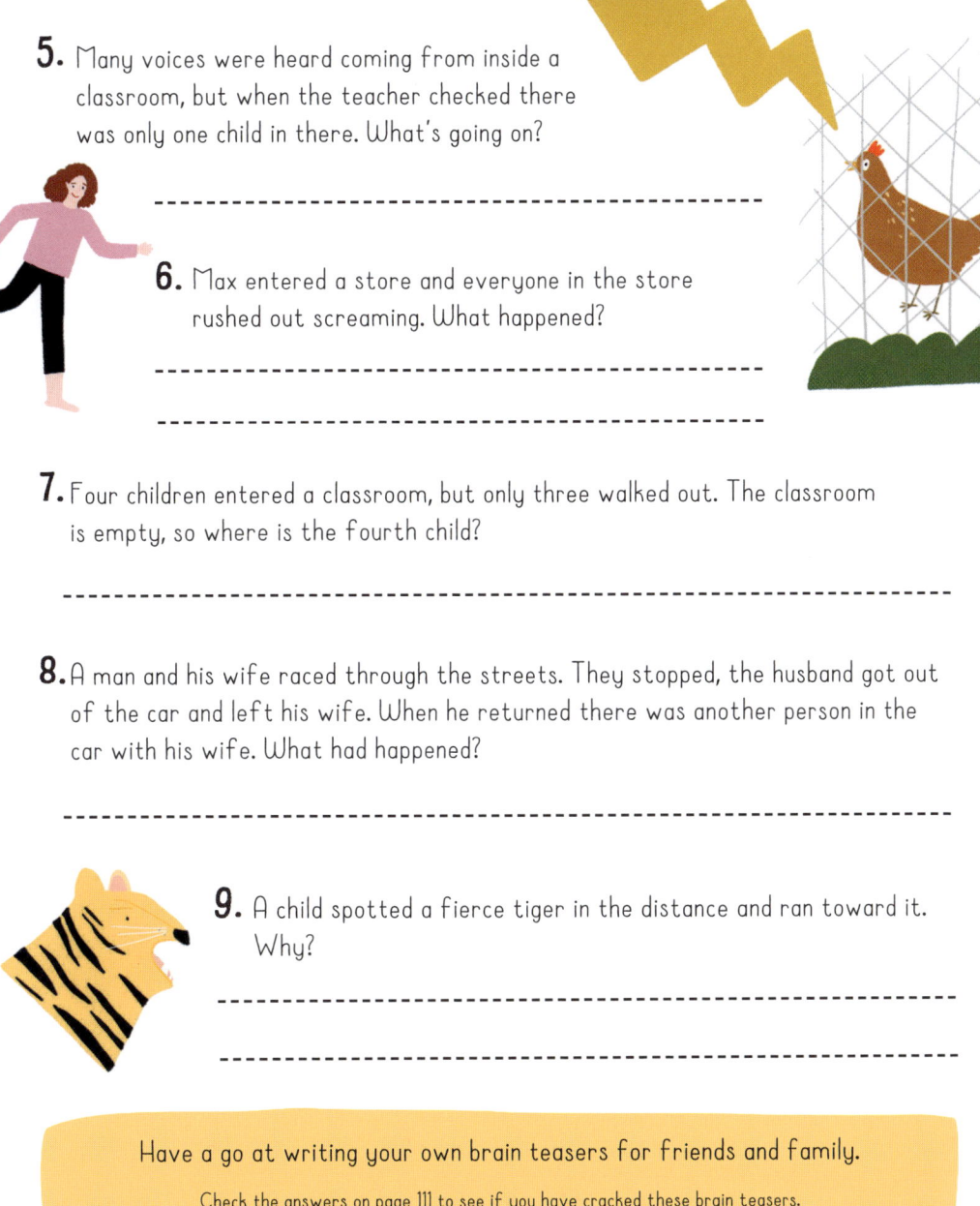

Have a go at writing your own brain teasers for friends and family.

Check the answers on page 111 to see if you have cracked these brain teasers.

"Where there's hope, there's life. It fills us with fresh courage and makes us strong again."

— Anne Frank

Let your mind wander, and fill this space with your notes, ideas, and doodles.

HOT COLORS

Summon your inner dragon power to color this fire-breathing dragon.

SAY NO TO BULLIES

Bullying is when someone is hurt on more than one occasion by another person or a group of people. It can include physical harm, name-calling, spreading gossip and lies about someone, and online bullying. It takes courage to stand up to bullies, whether you are the victim, or a bystander who can see it happening to someone else.

IF YOU ARE BEING BULLIED

Bullying is serious as it can be hurtful and disrupt people's lives, causing long-lasting pain. Victims of bullying may feel anxious and vulnerable and may get depressed and have trouble sleeping and eating. If you are being bullied here are some things you can do:

- Remember: it is not your fault and you have done nothing wrong.
- If it feels possible, tell an adult as soon as possible.
- If you are being verbally bullied do not respond to any hurtful insults. Try to remove yourself from the situation or tell the bully to stop in a strong, calm voice. Practice this with friends so you have some short simple phrases you might feel comfortable using.
- A bully is often looking for a big reaction, so try not to give one as this can make the situation worse. Once you are in a calm space you can express your hurt and rage to someone you trust.
- If the bullying feels physical, walk away to a safe space where you can be seen and heard by others. Bullies often choose places to be unkind to others where they think their behavior won't be noticed.

IF YOU SEE SOMEONE BEING BULLIED

Find your courage and speak up for someone you see being bullied, as they may be too afraid to do this. If it is safe to do so, tell the bully their behavior is wrong and hurtful. If necessary, go with the victim and talk to a trusted adult.

TAKE CARE WITH YOUR WORDS AND ACTIONS

Think about the words you use. Sometimes we may not realize that our words are hurtful to others. For example, if we make fun of someone, we may think that we are being funny, but the person we are making fun of may not feel that way and may be hurt by our words. It's okay to joke around, but be mindful of how your words affect others.

WHY DON'T YOU…

…Make an anti-bullying poster for your class, club, or home to show that it is not a place for bullies. Write some words and phrases in different colors, sizes, and styles. You can also add some doodles.

Here are some words and phrases you might use:

UPSTANDERS NOT BYSTANDERS

Don't suffer in silence

Acceptance

SPOT IT AND STOP IT!

BULLYING IS WRONG

BE KIND

Love

RESPECT

DARE TO BE DIFFERENT

We are all different and unique. Being different is good as it makes our planet interesting. What is unique about you? Do you have a special talent? Is it something you do, or the way you look, or the way you lead your life? Being different is your superpower. Sometimes it takes courage to own your superpower and stand out from the crowd.

Celebrate how special we all are by making some badges for you, your friends and family. Fill in what makes each of you special.

I'm proud to be
_____

My superpower is
_____
_____

I'm proud to be
_____

My superpower is
_____
_____

Color in and decorate the text.

COURAGEOUS ROLE MODELS
Be inspired by these courageous role models.

Name: Anne Frank
Born: 1929, Germany
Role: diary writer, who became a symbol of the Holocaust

Anne's story:
Anne and her family were Jewish. When Anne was growing up the ruling Nazis unjustly blamed the Jewish people for all the problems in Germany and introduced laws that made life difficult for them. When Anne's sister Margot was ordered to leave and go to a work camp, the whole family went into hiding along with four other people. Their hiding place was cramped, and Anne had to keep very quiet and was often scared. She passed the time writing a diary about what it was like hiding away and about her feelings, hopes, and dreams. Sadly, after almost two years the hideaways were discovered by the Nazis and taken away. By the end of the war, Anne's father Otto was the only survivor from the group.

Giving back: Otto decided to publish Anne's diary, *The Secret Annex*, as it shows Anne's extraordinary spirit and is an important record of this dreadful time in history known as the Holocaust. Their hideaway was also turned into a museum, called The Anne Frank House.

Name: Martin Luther King Jr
Born: 1929, America
Role: Baptist minister and civil-rights activist

Martin's story:
Martin Luther King Jr had a dream that all people would be equal. The problem was at the time when Martin was growing up in Alabama, black and white people were treated differently because of the color of their skin. For example, black people had to sit at the back of buses and give up their seats if there were no seats left for white people. Martin was a peaceful man and wrote letters, newspaper articles, and books, and organized marches to persuade people to end the unfair treatment of black people. His most famous speech was at a march in Washington in 1963, where he talked about his hopes and dreams of a world where people were equal.

Giving back: Martin Luther King Jr made people aware of the injustices faced by black people and inspired people to take action. In 1964 a law was made in America that banned treating people differently because of their color, race, or religion.

Name: Deng Adut
Born: About 1983, South Sudan
Role: child soldier, now a criminal lawyer

Deng's story:
War broke out in South Sudan where Deng lived, and at six years old he was snatched by soldiers and taken away to be trained as a child soldier. Conditions were tough, without much food and the children were roughly treated. Children who didn't obey orders were shot and many died from diseases. Deng met his older brother, who had also been snatched earlier. His brother helped Deng to escape by hiding him under some sacks in a truck and driving them to safety. With help, they eventually got to Australia as refugees. Deng studied hard to learn the language and make something of his life in his new home country, and became a lawyer. Sadly, Deng's brother was killed in Sudan when he went back to help people there.

Giving back: Deng set up a group that helps other refugees like him with their education in Australia, and he speaks out for justice in South Sudan. He also wrote a book about his experiences, which showed that despite a terrible childhood, he had the strength to carry on and make something of his life.

Name: Boyan Slat
Born: 1994, the Netherlands
Role: inventor and founder of The Ocean Cleanup

Boyan's story:
When sixteen-year-old Boyan Slat was on holiday in Greece with his family, he went scuba diving and noticed that there were more plastic bags in the ocean than fish. He was shocked to find out that plastic pollution in oceans and rivers was a worldwide problem and no one was doing anything to clean it up. He was determined to find a solution. After leaving school, Boyan set up a company called The Ocean Cleanup. After years of experimenting, they made a giant floating barrier to go in the ocean and catch passing pieces of plastic. Unfortunately, the barrier couldn't hold onto any plastic it caught and the plastic slipped back into the ocean, and strong waves broke the barrier in two. Boyan and his team didn't let these set backs stop them and worked on making a new, better barrier. The new barrier is now working well to clean up a polluted part of the Pacific Ocean. But this is only a tiny start to cleaning up the world's polluted oceans.

Giving back: Boyan started the largest ocean clean-up in history. All the plastic the barrier removes from the ocean is recycled and made into other products. Boyan has shown how to achieve things by keeping a positive outlook and turning challenges into opportunities to learn.

TRUE OR FALSE?

After working your way through this book, hopefully you will have a clearer idea of courage and can help to bust these myths. Join the myth-busters and write some reasons why each of these myths about courage is not true. Look back in this book if you need a reminder. The first one has been done for you. Once you have finished press the Bin-It button and say out loud "You are not true."

Courage and fear are opposites.
This is not true. Courage and fear always go together, as without fear there is no need for courage. Some of the most courageous people can be scared. Having courage is doing something brave even though you are scared.

Courage is climbing Mount Everest.

Courage isn't shown in everyday life.

Courage is something you are born with and not something you can learn.

If you are brave you are not scared.

There are no wrong answers if you can argue your point. However, look on page 111 for examples of some myth-busting reasons.

"Never bend your head. Always hold it high. Look the world straight in the eye."

– Helen Keller

Let your mind wander and fill this space with notes, ideas and doodles.

MY COURAGE DIARY

Use these next four pages to write about all the courageous things you have achieved this week.

DAY	ACTS OF COURAGE
	....
	....
	....
	....
	....
	....
	....
	....
	....
	....
	....
	....

DAY	ACTS OF COURAGE

DAY	ACTS OF COURAGE

COURAGE AWARDS

Give yourself and a friend or family member each a Courage Award. Write your names on the certificates and the most courageous thing you have each done.

COURAGE AWARD

To:

For:

I AM BRAVE

COURAGE AWARD

To:

For:

I AM BRAVE

CHECK YOUR ANSWERS

Brain teasers on pages 88-89:
1. The carrot, scarf, and four stones belonged to a snowman. But all the snow has melted leaving behind the carrot, scarf, and stones.
2. The woman's two sons were part of a set of triplets.
3. The man is very short and can only reach up to the tenth floor elevator button.
4. The lady was driving a bumper car at the fair.
5. The other voices were coming from a television, or a radio, or computer.
6. Max was a python who had escaped from the local zoo.
7. The fourth child is in a wheelchair, so they rolled out of the room instead of walking out.
8. The man's wife had a baby in the car whilst he had rushed inside the hospital to get help.
9. The child was at a wildlife park, and the tiger was in a fenced-off area.

Myths on pages 102-103:
- **Courage and fear are opposites.**
  This is not true. Courage and fear always go together, as without fear there is no need for courage. Having courage is doing something brave even though you are scared.
- **Courage is climbing Mount Everest.**
  This statement is too general. It does take courage to climb Mount Everest, but less dramatic things such as standing up for a friend or asking for help are also courageous. Look back through this book at different types of courage.
- **Courage isn't shown in everyday life.**
  This is not true. You can show courage every day of your life. Look back through this book at different types of courage.
- **Courage is something you are born with and not something you can learn.**
  This is not true. If you struggle with your fears and want to be more courageous, there are many ways that you can work on building your courage.
- **If you are brave you are not scared.**
  This is not true. Being brave is doing things even though you are scared. The bravest people are often scared but they don't let their fears hold them back from exploring new opportunities, developing their skills, and doing what is right.

FURTHER RESOURCES

Check out these links to find out even more information about emotions and mental health.

www.actionforhappiness.org
www.seizetheawkward.org
www.youngminds.org.uk
www.childmind.org
www.thetrevorproject.org
www.atlasofemotions.org
www.kooth.com
www.headspace.com

You can also contact a free and confidential helpline that is available online or by phone, such as:

Childhelp
(1-800) 422-4453
www.childhelp.org

Crisis text line
Text 741741
www.crisistextline.org

Stomp out bullying
www.stompoutbullying.org